TIMESHEET

LOG BOOK

Name: ______________________

Phone: ______________________

Name:	Month/Year:

Day	Date		Time In	Time Out	Total Hours

Name:	Month/Year:

Day	Date		Time In	Time Out	Total Hours

Name:	Month/Year:

Day	Date		Time In	Time Out	Total Hours

Name:	Month/Year:

Day	Date		Time In	Time Out	Total Hours

Name:	Month/Year:

Day	Date		Time In	Time Out	Total Hours

Name:	Month/Year:

Day	Date		Time In	Time Out	Total Hours

Name: **Month/Year:**

Day	Date		Time In	Time Out	Total Hours

Name:	Month/Year:

Day	Date		Time In	Time Out	Total Hours

Name:	Month/Year:

Day	Date		Time In	Time Out	Total Hours

Name:	Month/Year:

Day	Date		Time In	Time Out	Total Hours

Name:	Month/Year:

Day	Date		Time In	Time Out	Total Hours

Name:	Month/Year:

Day	Date		Time In	Time Out	Total Hours

Name:	Month/Year:

Day	Date		Time In	Time Out	Total Hours

Name:	Month/Year:

Day	Date		Time In	Time Out	Total Hours

Name:	Month/Year:

Day	Date		Time In	Time Out	Total Hours

Name:	Month/Year:

Day	Date		Time In	Time Out	Total Hours

Name:	Month/Year:

Day	Date		Time In	Time Out	Total Hours

Name:	Month/Year:

Day	Date		Time In	Time Out	Total Hours

Name:	**Month/Year:**

Day	Date		Time In	Time Out	Total Hours

Name:	Month/Year:

Day	Date		Time In	Time Out	Total Hours

Name:	Month/Year:

Day	Date		Time In	Time Out	Total Hours

Name:	Month/Year:

Day	Date		Time In	Time Out	Total Hours

Name:	Month/Year:

Day	Date		Time In	Time Out	Total Hours

Name:	Month/Year:

Day	Date		Time In	Time Out	Total Hours

Name:	Month/Year:

Day	Date		Time In	Time Out	Total Hours

Name:	Month/Year:

Day	Date		Time In	Time Out	Total Hours

Name:	Month/Year:

Day	Date		Time In	Time Out	Total Hours

Name:	Month/Year:

Day	Date		Time In	Time Out	Total Hours

Name:	Month/Year:

Day	Date		Time In	Time Out	Total Hours

Name:	Month/Year:

Day	Date		Time In	Time Out	Total Hours

Name:	Month/Year:

Day	Date		Time In	Time Out	Total Hours

Name:	Month/Year:

Day	Date		Time In	Time Out	Total Hours

Name:	Month/Year:

Day	Date		Time In	Time Out	Total Hours

Name:	Month/Year:

Day	Date		Time In	Time Out	Total Hours

Name:	Month/Year:

Day	Date		Time In	Time Out	Total Hours

Name:	Month/Year:

Day	Date		Time In	Time Out	Total Hours

Name:	Month/Year:

Day	Date		Time In	Time Out	Total Hours

Name:	Month/Year:

Day	Date		Time In	Time Out	Total Hours

Name:	Month/Year:

Day	Date		Time In	Time Out	Total Hours

Name:	Month/Year:

Day	Date		Time In	Time Out	Total Hours

Name:	Month/Year:

Day	Date		Time In	Time Out	Total Hours

Name:	Month/Year:

Day	Date		Time In	Time Out	Total Hours

Name:	Month/Year:

Day	Date		Time In	Time Out	Total Hours

Name:	Month/Year:

Day	Date		Time In	Time Out	Total Hours

Name:	Month/Year:

Day	Date		Time In	Time Out	Total Hours

Name:	Month/Year:

Day	Date		Time In	Time Out	Total Hours

Name:	Month/Year:

Day	Date		Time In	Time Out	Total Hours

Name:	Month/Year:

Day	Date		Time In	Time Out	Total Hours

Name:	Month/Year:

Day	Date		Time In	Time Out	Total Hours

Name:	Month/Year:

Day	Date		Time In	Time Out	Total Hours

Name:	Month/Year:

Day	Date		Time In	Time Out	Total Hours

Name:	Month/Year:

Day	Date		Time In	Time Out	Total Hours

Name:	Month/Year:

Day	Date		Time In	Time Out	Total Hours

Name:	Month/Year:

Day	Date		Time In	Time Out	Total Hours

Name:	Month/Year:

Day	Date		Time In	Time Out	Total Hours

Name:	Month/Year:

Day	Date		Time In	Time Out	Total Hours

Name:	Month/Year:

Day	Date		Time In	Time Out	Total Hours

Name:	Month/Year:

Day	Date		Time In	Time Out	Total Hours

Name:	Month/Year:

Day	Date		Time In	Time Out	Total Hours

Name:	Month/Year:

Day	Date		Time In	Time Out	Total Hours

Name:	Month/Year:

Day	Date		Time In	Time Out	Total Hours

Name:	Month/Year:

Day	Date		Time In	Time Out	Total Hours

Name:	Month/Year:

Day	Date		Time In	Time Out	Total Hours

Name:	Month/Year:

Day	Date		Time In	Time Out	Total Hours

Name:	Month/Year:

Day	Date		Time In	Time Out	Total Hours

Name:	Month/Year:

Day	Date		Time In	Time Out	Total Hours

Name:	Month/Year:

Day	Date		Time In	Time Out	Total Hours

Name:	Month/Year:

Day	Date		Time In	Time Out	Total Hours

Name:	Month/Year:

Day	Date		Time In	Time Out	Total Hours

Name:	**Month/Year:**

Day	Date		Time In	Time Out	Total Hours

Name:	Month/Year:

Day	Date		Time In	Time Out	Total Hours

Name:	Month/Year:

Day	Date		Time In	Time Out	Total Hours

Name:	Month/Year:

Day	Date		Time In	Time Out	Total Hours

Name:	Month/Year:

Day	Date		Time In	Time Out	Total Hours

Name:	Month/Year:

Day	Date		Time In	Time Out	Total Hours

Name:	Month/Year:

Day	Date		Time In	Time Out	Total Hours

Name:	Month/Year:

Day	Date		Time In	Time Out	Total Hours

Name:	Month/Year:

Day	Date		Time In	Time Out	Total Hours

Name:	Month/Year:

Day	Date		Time In	Time Out	Total Hours

Name:	Month/Year:

Day	Date		Time In	Time Out	Total Hours

Name:	Month/Year:

Day	Date		Time In	Time Out	Total Hours

Name:	Month/Year:

Day	Date		Time In	Time Out	Total Hours

Name:	Month/Year:

Day	Date		Time In	Time Out	Total Hours

Name:	Month/Year:

Day	Date		Time In	Time Out	Total Hours

Name:	Month/Year:

Day	Date		Time In	Time Out	Total Hours

Name:	Month/Year:

Day	Date		Time In	Time Out	Total Hours

Name:	Month/Year:

Day	Date		Time In	Time Out	Total Hours

Name:	Month/Year:

Day	Date		Time In	Time Out	Total Hours

Name:	Month/Year:

Day	Date		Time In	Time Out	Total Hours

Name:	Month/Year:

Day	Date		Time In	Time Out	Total Hours

Name:	Month/Year:

Day	Date		Time In	Time Out	Total Hours

Name:	Month/Year:

Day	Date		Time In	Time Out	Total Hours

Name:	Month/Year:

Day	Date		Time In	Time Out	Total Hours

Name:	Month/Year:

Day	Date		Time In	Time Out	Total Hours

Name:	Month/Year:

Day	Date		Time In	Time Out	Total Hours

Name:	Month/Year:

Day	Date		Time In	Time Out	Total Hours

Name: | **Month/Year:**

Day	Date		Time In	Time Out	Total Hours

Name:	Month/Year:

Day	Date		Time In	Time Out	Total Hours

USEFUL WORK CONTACTS

NAME	PHONE NO.	Details

MONTH:

SUNDAY	MONDAY	TUESDAY	WENDSDAY	THURSDAY	FRIDAY	SATURDAY

MONTH:

SUNDAY	MONDAY	TUESDAY	WENDSDAY	THURSDAY	FRIDAY	SATURDAY

MONTH:

SUNDAY	MONDAY	TUESDAY	WENDSDAY	THURSDAY	FRIDAY	SATURDAY

MONTH:

SUNDAY	MONDAY	TUESDAY	WENDSDAY	THURSDAY	FRIDAY	SATURDAY

MONTH:

SUNDAY	MONDAY	TUESDAY	WENDSDAY	THURSDAY	FRIDAY	SATURDAY

MONTH:

SUNDAY	MONDAY	TUESDAY	WENDSDAY	THURSDAY	FRIDAY	SATURDAY

MONTH:

SUNDAY	MONDAY	TUESDAY	WENDSDAY	THURSDAY	FRIDAY	SATURDAY

MONTH:

SUNDAY	MONDAY	TUESDAY	WENDSDAY	THURSDAY	FRIDAY	SATURDAY

MONTH:

SUNDAY	MONDAY	TUESDAY	WENDSDAY	THURSDAY	FRIDAY	SATURDAY

MONTH:

SUNDAY	MONDAY	TUESDAY	WENDSDAY	THURSDAY	FRIDAY	SATURDAY

MONTH:

SUNDAY	MONDAY	TUESDAY	WENDSDAY	THURSDAY	FRIDAY	SATURDAY

MONTH:

SUNDAY	MONDAY	TUESDAY	WENDSDAY	THURSDAY	FRIDAY	SATURDAY

MONTH: ....

SUNDAY	MONDAY	TUESDAY	WENDSDAY	THURSDAY	FRIDAY	SATURDAY

MONTH: ....

SUNDAY	MONDAY	TUESDAY	WENDSDAY	THURSDAY	FRIDAY	SATURDAY

MONTH: ....

SUNDAY	MONDAY	TUESDAY	WENDSDAY	THURSDAY	FRIDAY	SATURDAY

MONTH: ....

SUNDAY	MONDAY	TUESDAY	WENDSDAY	THURSDAY	FRIDAY	SATURDAY

MONTH: ....

SUNDAY	MONDAY	TUESDAY	WENDSDAY	THURSDAY	FRIDAY	SATURDAY

MONTH: ....

SUNDAY	MONDAY	TUESDAY	WENDSDAY	THURSDAY	FRIDAY	SATURDAY

MONTH: ....

SUNDAY	MONDAY	TUESDAY	WENDSDAY	THURSDAY	FRIDAY	SATURDAY

MONTH: ....

SUNDAY	MONDAY	TUESDAY	WENDSDAY	THURSDAY	FRIDAY	SATURDAY

MONTH: ....

SUNDAY	MONDAY	TUESDAY	WENDSDAY	THURSDAY	FRIDAY	SATURDAY

MONTH: ....

SUNDAY	MONDAY	TUESDAY	WENDSDAY	THURSDAY	FRIDAY	SATURDAY

MONTH: ....

SUNDAY	MONDAY	TUESDAY	WENDSDAY	THURSDAY	FRIDAY	SATURDAY

MONTH: ....

SUNDAY	MONDAY	TUESDAY	WENDSDAY	THURSDAY	FRIDAY	SATURDAY

Notes

Notes

Notes

Made in the USA
Monee, IL
28 October 2024

68809041R00059